Scorpio

23 October – 21 November

D1607761

amber
BOOKS

ASTROLOGICAL SIGN DATES:
The precise start and end times for each sign vary by a day or two from year to year as the Gregorian calendar shifts relative to the tropical year. The dates provided in this book are correct for the year 2020.

If you are unsure of the Zodiac sign for your specific birth year, visit: www.yourzodiacsign.com.

Scorpio

23 October – 21 November

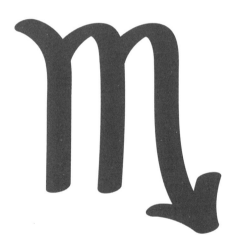

A guide to understanding yourself, your
friendships and finding your true love

This edition first published in 2020 by
Amber Books Ltd
United House
North Road
London N7 9DP
United Kingdom
www.amberbooks.co.uk
Instagram: amberbooksltd
Facebook: amberbooks
Twitter: @amberbooks

ISBN: 978-1-83886-030-1

Project Editor: Sarah Uttridge
Design: Zoë Mellors

Picture Credits:
All illustrations by Fabbri Publications except the following:
Shutterstock: 31 (Elena Naumchenkova), 32 (La Puma), 35 (Slonomysh),
36 (Angel Soler Gollonet)

Printed and bound in China

TRADITIONAL CHINESE BOOKBINDING
This book has been produced using traditional Chinese bookbinding
techniques, using a method that was developed during the Ming Dynasty
(1368–1644) and remained in use until the adoption of Western binding
techniques in the early 1900s. In traditional Chinese binding, single sheets
of paper are printed on one side only, and each sheet is folded in half,
with the printed pages on the outside. The book block is then sandwiched
between two boards and sewn together through punched holes close to
the cut edges of the folded sheets.

Contents

Introduction

Scorpio

23 October–21 November

Sign: The Scorpion

Ruling Planets: Mars and Pluto

Gender: Feminine

Element: Water

Quality: Fixed

Compatibility: Taurus, Virgo and Libra

Non-compatibility: Aries, Leo and Sagittarius

Every man, woman and child is born with a distinct and different destiny. There are no exceptions. Everyone has cosmic significance and a part to play in the life of the universe. This is innate and inescapable, and goes beyond the tiny boundaries of nation, creed and colour.

As we live out our lives on planet Earth, we are, however unknowingly, acting in a greater drama and reacting to impulses that come from distant astronomical bodies, stars and planets millions of light years away. Sceptics pour scorn on the idea that far-distant Saturn, for example, can have any effect on our lives, as the ancient art and science of astrology teaches. But the fact is that we are sparks of energy inhabiting bodies made of the same stuff as the stars, responding like tiny radios to the distant messages they send to Earth.

Each infant carries within it a double blueprint for life: its genetic programming and the pattern of character that comes from the astrological 'clock' that was set in motion at the moment of birth. No one knows the full extent of genetic influence, although it seems to be astonishingly far-reaching, but the power of the horoscope has been well known to the wisest men and women for many centuries.

Our Sun and Moon signs provide essential inside information about our destinies. They reveal the secrets of who we really are, and why we are here, laying out before us our potential, the sort of joys and achievements our characteristics may bring about, and warn us of problems to be overcome through the triumph of free will.

Read this book with an open mind and discover who you really are.

The Elements

U p to the beginning of the Age of Enlightenment – the modern scientific era – in the 18th century, it was commonly believed that everything, including human beings, was made up of the four elements: Earth, Air, Fire and Water. These were thought of as the building blocks of life, and each astrological sign had a predominance of one or another. Each created its common characteristics, although too much of any of the elements can produce an unbalanced personality.

Water Signs

The Water signs are Cancer, Scorpio and Pisces. They are emotional, intuitive and often psychic, strongly in touch with the hidden, mysterious side of life and with the ebb and flow of unseen energies. Like the ocean tides, they have surges of inspiration and bursts of euphoria, or they can be plunged into gloom and introspection. Cancerians are emotionally tied to their homes and families; like their sign, the Crab, they jealously guard their own particular little rock pool, hiding their softest feelings under a hard shell.

Scorpians are the occultists and profound thinkers of the zodiac, very sexy and magnetic, but sometimes too intense. They are the still waters that run deep – very, very deep.

Pisceans' emotions can lie undisturbed for long periods, then suddenly rise to the surface. They can be fast and elusive – slippery customers, sometimes – and change direction for no apparent reason, often against their own best interests. But, like the other two Water signs, they operate almost entirely through their feelings, which can be very positive when set against the dour practicality of a Capricornian or the most reliable investment banker of a Taurean. They give depth to the adventures of the Arian and the madcap schemes of the Geminian, and reveal some of the mysteries of the Universe, which is never a bad thing.

Water Signs

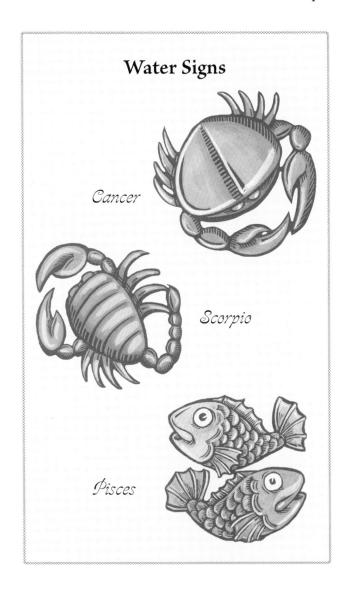

Cancer

Scorpio

Pisces

Colours
of the Zodiac

Traditionally, each sign of the zodiac has its own colour, which is believed to be 'lucky' or magically empowered for those born under that particular sign. In general, the colours are associated with the ruling planets and are symbolic of their attributes. Many people find that they feel most comfortable when wearing their sign's colours, and often choose them without knowing their full astrological background.

Scorpio

Ruling Planet: Pluto.

Colours: Black and red. Dramatic, uncompromising and sexy, these are 'dangerous' colours, especially when used together.

The Angelic Hierarchy

According to ancient tradition, each planet is governed by one of the great archangels, who also rule aspects of human life. The box below lists the planet that they govern, the areas they influence and their day of the week.

Azrael

Archangel of Pluto.

Governs: Scorpio.

Rules: Death and rebirth, the mysteries of the afterlife and karma, and buried treasure.

Day: Azrael is not associated with any particular day.

The Genders

Traditionally, the twelve signs of the zodiac are divided into Masculine and Feminine, although of course both men and women are born into each.

The characteristics were assigned to the genders aeons ago, well before modern feminism or political correctness, and may now seem old-fashioned to many. However, the signs do seem to be grouped according to the appropriate gender.

The Feminine Signs

The Feminine signs are Taurus, Cancer, Virgo, Scorpio, Capricorn and Pisces. Feminine traits tend to be most accentuated in the Water signs of Cancer and Pisces.

These signs present gentler, more passive qualities. They are the carers and the nurturers, inclined to take a back seat and worry over the well-being of others. They are artistic and in tune with their intuition, and may be psychic. Self-evidently, these are the motherly and sisterly signs, with all the attendant positive and negative characteristics. They tend to be the power behind the throne, rather than movers and shakers, although many are great achievers, especially in the modern, more egalitarian world, where their qualities are encouraged.

Negatively, the Feminine signs can be fussy, possessive, mean-minded, vindictive, cringing, clinging and over-emotional.

Aquarius, the sign of the coming Age, is endowed with both Masculine and Feminine traits, although it is traditionally categorized as Masculine.

The Ruling Planets

Until the 18th century, astrologers knew only the planets of our solar system that could be seen with the naked eye: Mercury, Venus, Mars, Jupiter and Saturn. (For the purposes of astrology, the Sun and the Moon are also counted as planets, even though the Sun is a star and the Moon is the satellite of Earth.) Uranus was discovered in 1781, Neptune in 1846 and Pluto was first seen in 1930. Many astrologers believe that the existence of other heavenly bodies – such as the rumoured Vulcan, which hypothetically exists within the orbit of Mercury – is about to be confirmed. Astrologers will then have to agree which signs these 'new' planets will rule, and what human characteristics their discovery will accentuate.

Mars

Mars was the Roman god of war, from whom we derive our word 'martial'.

Arians are ruled by war-like Mars, as are Scorpians (although the latter are now also ruled by Pluto). Mars gives Aries its fiery zeal, its courage that often amounts to foolhardiness and its explosive temper. It bestows on Scorpio its red-blooded sense of drama and angry passion.

About Mars

Mars is the fourth planet beyond the Sun. Due to its extremely elliptical orbit, Mars can pass as close to the Sun as 208 million km (129 million miles), and takes 687 days to circle it.

Tuesday is sacred to Mars.

About Pluto

Pluto is about 4800 km (3000 miles) across and 5800 million km (3600 million miles) from the Sun, which it circles at a rate of once every 248 years.

There is no day sacred to Pluto but, by association with Mars, Tuesday could be eligible. Saturday, the day of Saturn, is also a contender.

Pluto

Pluto was named after the Greco-Roman god who ruled the Underworld. It is associated with the unconscious mind, with secrets and karmic liabilities. With Mars, the ninth planet now co-rules Scorpio, endowing that sign with its passion for the occult and for plumbing the depths of the human psyche.

The Qualities

In addition to the influence of gender, the elements and the planets, each sign of the zodiac is affected by having an intrinsic quality – Cardinal, Fixed or Mutable.

Fixed Quality

Individuals born under a Fixed sign have an inherent disposition towards tradition, convention and stability. They hate change and often refuse to adapt to new circumstances. These people are not happy taking the initiative or being in situations that require a quick-fire response. Fixed signs also tend to have conventional, conservative opinions and find it hard to move with the times. However, they do tend to be reliable and down to earth.

Scorpio

Although highly emotional, those born under this Water sign know their own mind and react strongly, even violently, against challenges to their position. Many of their opinions were formed when young and will remain the basis for much of their adult decision-making. Often unable to adapt or see alternative points of view, Scorpians take everything very personally.

Signs and Symbols

Most people are familiar with the zodiac 'zoo' – the collection of symbols that represent the twelve signs. These images reflect the characteristics traditionally assigned to each sign and contain a wealth of knowledge about its true nature.

Each sign of the zodiac is represented by a symbol – the twin fish for Pisces, for example. No one is sure exactly when or why the symbols were chosen, although some authorities believe they date from Sumeria or Mesopotamia, 4000 years before Jesus Christ. The priest-astrologers of the ancient world were the first to impose recognizable patterns on the great constellations – Leo the Lion being one example.

Today, seeing such shapes in the stars may seem fanciful, but thousands of years ago imaginations were more poetic, and many myths told of magical animals, such as the dragon, which had strange powers to influence everyday human life.

Although the ancient Egyptians left few astrological records, they were almost unique in antiquity for worshipping archetypal, animal-headed gods. However, these strange hybrid gods – half-human, half-animal – were worshipped as aspects of one God. Contrary to the general belief that the Egyptians were idolaters, their religion was basically monotheistic. Each statue represented an aspect of the one true God.

Since they were established, the signs have remained unchanged, although there was a movement in the Middle Ages to change the sign of Aquarius to the sign of John the Baptist – presumably because of the connection with water.

The twelve signs of the zodiac do seem particularly apt on the whole, and accurately reflect the archetypal character of Sun sign types. The great Swiss psychoanalyst Carl Gustav Jung (1875–1961) believed that, deep in our psyches, humanity shares a collective unconscious – a set of archetypal images, which, at a profound level, we all understand. The signs of the zodiac form part of this pool of images, conveying eternal truths to our unconscious minds.

Signs and Symbols

Aries

Taurus

Gemini

Cancer

Leo

Virgo

Libra

Scorpio

Sagittarius

Capricorn

Aquarius

Pisces

Scorpio
The Scorpion

These tiny, armoured creatures are greatly feared, yet few of them possess a sting that is serious, let alone fatal. Image is all to a Scorpian. Sometimes, however, they are so eager to attack enemies with their venom that they overreach and actually sting themselves. This should act as a dire warning to vengeful, dark-hearted Scorpian types.

Originally, the symbol for this sign was the Phoenix, the magical bird of mythology, which was consumed in fire, only to rise from the ashes, as magnificent as ever. This is very much the positive side of Scorpio.

There are many mythological and magical associations with the Phoenix. He was intimately involved with the transformative aspects of alchemy, and often represented the cycle of incarnation, death and rebirth. The Phoenix also, occasionally, symbolized the many dying-and-rising gods of the ancient world. These included Attis, Osiris, Tammuz, Adonis, Dionysus, Mithras and, last of all, Jesus. Their deaths were associated with the coming of winter, and their rebirth with the renewal of nature in the spring, and with reincarnation. Every year, there were great festivals to celebrate the death and resurrection of these gods. These were eventually appropriated by the early Church and became the Christian celebration of Easter.

The Sun in Scorpio

Sun sign Scorpians are energetic, passionate and exciting. They have often had a negative reputation among traditional astrologers, but fortunately relatively few live up to their somewhat unsavoury image. Most Scorpians content themselves with being forceful and fascinating, dramatically sweeping through the lives of others like mini-tornadoes. Of course, there are those born under the sign of the Scorpion who seem shy and retiring, but they are few and far between. Even then they will tend to harbour deep, dark secrets, for this sign is nothing if not mysterious.

Most Scorpians have a strong sex drive, which may express itself in endless flirting or even power games. Often, though, it is sublimated in a quest for the Great Mission In Life, for finding their personal Holy Grail or plumbing the mysteries of life.

Ruled by Pluto, god of the Underworld, Scorpians are concerned with esoteric matters, with the paranormal, mysticism and the afterlife, and often believe passionately in reincarnation. This is not always as negative as it may sound: Scorpians understand the concept that death is always followed by rebirth, and they can rise like the Phoenix from disastrous events in their own lives to start again with enormous positive energy. Disappointment, bereavement, bankruptcy, illness and natural disasters can depress and seem, at the time, to demolish them, but not for long. Soon they are back on their feet, building new lives for themselves and others with amazing cheerfulness and genuine joy at being given the opportunity for a fresh start.

Personality Traits of Scorpians

Positive	*Negative*
Energetic	Unsettling
Passionate	Forceful
Flirtatious	Jealous
Exciting	Possessive
Outrageous	Sarcastic
Fascinating	Love to shock
Persistent	Mysterious
Loyal	Secretive

Sun sign Scorpians have a marked tendency to jealousy and possessiveness. Profoundly secretive by nature, they can often disturb others with their air of mystery, which can sometimes seem just a little contrived. Scorpians are very theatrical, and can use every trick in the book to get noticed at social gatherings: they love to be outrageous and to shock, which they often do very successfully, just for the hell of it.

However, there is a sting in the tail with Scorpians. The full Scorpian fury can be unsettling enough – after all, their other ruler is fiery, aggressive Mars – but to be on the receiving end of their cold, penetrating sarcasm is to be upset for days. Many Scorpians train themselves to be masters of the put-down that is devastatingly witty but hurtful.

Scorpio is a sign of extremes, of black and white, dark and light; this is often reflected in the ups and downs of their lives. These people can be wildly successful one year and bankrupt the next, although this is a process that is likely to be repeated in a curiously predictable cycle. Similarly, Scorpians can be utterly loyal and true lovers, but their great passion can rapidly turn to hatred and maybe even a desire for revenge.

Appearance

Once seen, rarely forgotten, Sun sign Scorpians are always striking, whether they are stunningly beautiful or not. They have a magnetic, forceful quality that makes people stare, although they may not be sure why. Most Scorpians have a habit of staring penetratingly, and of frowning while listening to others talk. They can move slowly, as if mesmerized, although their thought processes

are extremely fast. Even when dressing scruffily – and many often do – there is a certain style about them, a bohemian air that makes all the difference. Some work at it, but many find it comes naturally. This is definitely the sign of big hats and black coats. Scorpians are also very partial to wearing leather.

Health

The Scorpio motto is 'What the Hell ...' so, to them, moderation in anything is for wimps. They throw themselves into orgies of eating and drinking that would shame a Taurean, and often think that they somehow avert the day of reckoning

by doing it in style, drinking only champagne, for example, or eating only the best bitter chocolate. But whatever the quality, their lifestyle will catch up with them (usually sooner rather than later) in the shape of stomach trouble, chronic constipation, gall stones, liver and kidney problems, even diabetes. A shocking health scare, however, can be an abrupt turning point for Scorpio, whose ability to live at either end of the spectrum can turn them overnight into the most zealous, proselytizing, non-smoking teetotaller or the strictest vegan. Similarly, they can go from sybaritic couch potato to marathon runner just as easily, and enjoy both lifestyles with equal gusto.

Traditionally, Scorpians are supposed to suffer from genital problems, and of course some do. But in many cases this is transposed to lower back pain, often caused by too much sitting around and weight gain in middle age.

Career

'The Devil finds work for idle hands' was never truer than in the case of an out-of-work Scorpian, whose enormous energy needs to be positively channelled, or they may turn to dubious ways of passing the time – for instance, playing around with the Ouija board. However, once a Scorpian is fully engaged emotionally, there are few more energetic or ambitious workers. They are keen to throw themselves into what is right for them, often working through the night without any idea of the time. It is often said that they are fanatical money-grabbers. They certainly have that potential, but mostly they see money as an outward and visible sign of their dominance in their chosen field, of dramatic success compared to lesser mortals. If their work does not appeal to them, though, they can easily be sackably sloppy and lazy.

Scorpians are traditionally associated with jobs that require delving and uncovering secrets, such as mining and detective work, but few actually take up such professions. However, Scorpians tend to have more interesting, even peculiar, jobs than most because of their fascination with anything deep and dark. For example, they can be criminologists or forensic scientists working on murder cases for the police, or writers of detective fiction. Many carve out successful careers in the police force. They can be drawn to 'alternative' studies, such as parapsychology, the occult, ancient Egyptian mysteries or piecing together the truth about religion. Many are passionate about conspiracy theories. Even if they have humdrum everyday jobs, Scorpians tend to follow hobbies that reflect their

The best careers for Scorpians

- Forensic scientist
- Criminologist
- Crime writer
- Hypnotherapist
- Chemist
- Researcher
- Psychotherapist

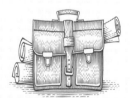

unusual, even bizarre, interests, and they may often find more ordinary people too boring for words.

The Scorpian need to go deep also makes them excellent counsellors and psychotherapists. Scorpians are at home with the unconscious mind, and are less fearful than most people about discovering its dark secrets. They can also find ingenious ways of coping with them.

Scorpians can be disruptive in the workplace. They take criticism so personally and react with such black and brooding moods, perhaps even flying into dramatic rages, that other, more timid souls will steer clear of them, even when teamwork suffers. They see everything – status, pay and perks – as a reflection of their own worth, and can make formidable rivals. If crossed, Scorpians can be very unforgiving.

They can make demanding bosses but, if their emotions are fully engaged, they can be surprisingly sympathetic and loyal to employees, taking any of their problems or setbacks as a personal challenge. Many Scorpians find life easier when self-employed, although they do like to have regular contact with others. They also need to feel that they are making their mark on the world. Too much time alone can make Scorpians very gloomy.

Relationships

Intense, sexual and demanding, Scorpians are not easy to live with. They are not above using sex as a form of control, although they don't indulge in emotional blackmail as much as Cancerians. Many Scorpians are much more interested in the image of sexual conquests than in the act itself.

Depending very much on other factors in the individual chart, Scorpians can throw all their energies into chasing often highly unsuitable people and will continue to pursue them when it is obvious that there is no point any more. They won't take no for an answer, refusing to believe that anyone could reject someone as fascinating and sexy as themselves. There is another element in this scenario, however. Scorpians often believe in fate or karma, and once they've got it in their heads that the object of their affections is meant for them, they ignore every indication to the contrary. Because of their tendency to use sexuality to control others, Scorpians see seduction as a form of possession, and believe that, however reluctant the object of their desire may be, one day their view will prevail. Often, though, they

are not as promiscuous as their reputation suggests and yearn to be involved in a passionate love affair that will transcend the humdrum world.

Scorpians can be very vindictive and vengeful. Never expect to walk away from a romance with a Scorpian unscathed. Not all Scorpians will necessarily bring down their full wrath upon those who have offended them – though they will fantasize about it.

They make demanding parents and can put too much pressure on their children. On the lighter side, though, they can be rather witty. Sometimes, Scorpians find it hard to give their children the necessary space to be themselves, and can be sticklers for tradition and discipline. Even so, they can learn to relax and be fun parents, so it is a good idea for them to participate in all sorts of activities with their children in order to lighten up.

Ideal Partner

Scorpians, with all their love of drama, may often be attracted to their own sign for that reason alone. It rarely works out, however, because of a Scorpian's temperamental nature and all the scenes that go with it. Also, there may not be enough real love.

Underneath a Scorpian's theatrical exterior is someone who just wants to be loved and to be made to feel normal. Their polar sign of Taurus can give them just what they crave – material and emotional security. Virgoans, too, share the ability to calm Scorpians and make them relax, often winning them over with their wit and charm. Well-balanced Librans also share the capacity to humour Scorpians and see beyond the image to the real, needy person inside. Arians, Leos and Sagittarians, however, can be too caught up in themselves to take the time to understand the complex Scorpian and are more likely to compete for the limelight. Scorpian leanings towards the world of the unexplained can make them gravitate towards the more psychic Pisceans, but it rarely works out because Scorpian intensity combined with Piscean emotionality is not a good recipe for enduring love.

Compatibility in Relationships

Aries
20 March–19 April

Arians may bring a breath of fresh air into the claustrophobic world of the Scorpian, but they can also be too demanding.

Capricorn
21 December–20 January

Capricornian repression has little appeal for sexually adventurous Scorpians and may lead to frostiness.

Cancer
21 June–21 July

Devoted Cancerians are too normal for quirky Scorpians, and their emotional highs and lows get short shrift.

Taurus
20 April–20 May

Perhaps curiously, Scorpio's opposite sign can prove very appealing and make a long-term relationship work well.

Libra
23 September–22 October

Scorpians often fascinate Librans and they can enjoy very passionate sex, but Scorpians are just too dark.

Leo
22 July–22 August

Relationships will be passionate and sex exciting but Scorpians do not take kindly to Leonine attempts to dominate.

Scorpio
23 October–21 November

Fellow Scorpians often get on well, having the same unusual interests, but may fall out of love too easily.

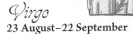

Virgo
23 August–22 September

The more sociable Virgoans can be complementary partners, but not if they embody the trait of Virgoan obsessive tidiness.

Aquarius
21 January–18 February

Scorpians often respect the causes espoused by Aquarians, but can find them too involved in 'boring' politics.

Sagittarius
22 November–20 December

Scorpians find these wild children very charming, but do not go for the insecurity or lack of permanent lifestyle.

Gemini
21 May–20 June

Flighty, wily Geminians can charm Scorpians, but not for long. In the end, they're just too shallow for Scorpio.

Pisces
19 February–19 March

Both signs are complex and intense with extreme demands. Lasting and loving relationships are unlikely.

The Scorpian Child

Scorpian children are natural loners, brooders and worriers. They like to sit alone pondering over very adult questions that can alarm their siblings and parents alike. They can become very religious at an early age, and although there may be nothing at all wrong with the belief system itself, they should be weaned away, gently and uncritically, into more active pursuits, and encouraged to play with other children. Yet it goes against the nature of Sun sign Scorpians to be completely open and 'natural'. They will always have their secrets and dark passions. Sometimes it does more harm than good to try to persuade a Scorpian child to join in more boisterous pursuits. So on the principle that if you can't beat them, join them, it might be a good idea to accompany them to the Egyptian galleries in the museum and investigate the mummies together.

When distressed or off-colour, Scorpians tend to go very quiet, retreating into their own world, to the bewilderment and hurt of their loved ones. They can bottle up all sorts of profound feelings – sometimes it is hard even to let their parents know what they want for a birthday present. Somehow they just can't articulate something so passionately desired, while knowing that if they say nothing, they are unlikely to get it. For their happiness and future health, they should be encouraged to open up and share at least some of their secret hopes and fears.

Although Scorpians often feel low and retreat into a gloom, they soon spring back into life. Because of their enormous reserves of energy and courage, and their capacity to recover quickly from both mental and physical illnesses, Scorpians are excellent people to have around in tough times. Once again, it is their underlying conviction that Fate is on their side that sees them through, and even as children, they can be surprisingly adult, suddenly snapping out of their introspection to take charge in an emergency.

Famous Scorpians

Prince Charles

Theodore Roosevelt

Marie Antoinette

Richard Burton

Edward III

August Rodin

Jamie Lee Curtis

Evelyn Waugh

Charles Atlas

Albert Camus

Stephen T. Crane

Marie Curie

François Mitterrand

Pablo Picasso

Vivien Leigh

Erwin Rommel

Martin Luther

Cheiro (Palmist)

George Patton

Paul Joseph Goebbels

Finding Your Sun Sign (2020 dates)

Aries	20 March–19 April*
Taurus	20 April–20 May
Gemini	21 May–20 June
Cancer	21 June–21 July
Leo	22 July–22 August
Virgo	23 August–22 September
Libra	23 September–22 October
Scorpio	23 October–21 November
Sagittarius	22 November–20 December
Capricorn	21 December–20 January
Aquarius	21 January–18 February
Pisces	19 February–19 March

*The dates provided in this book reflect the year 2020.
Dates may vary by a day or two from year to year.